Testing the Waters

A Poetry Collection

+ | +

KEVIN HASZTO

Testing the Waters: A Poetry Collection

Copyright ©2019 Kevin Haszto
All rights reserved. First edition 2019

No part of this book may be reproduced or transmitted in any form or by any means, electronic or mechanical, including photocopying, recording or by any information storage and retrieval system, without permission in writing from the publisher.

Produced in the United States of America

First Edition, paperback version
ISBN 978-1-73332-370-3

1. Self-realization—Poetry. 2. Spiritual life—Poetry.

Published by SageSong Press LLC
email: sagesongpress@gmail.com

Printed by Lulu.com in the United States

Cover Design and Photography by Kevin Haszto. Photograph is the bay view from Robert Moses State Park, Long Island, NY

This book is dedicated to my loving parents
Paul and Stella Haszto, whom always encouraged me
and gave me freedom to find and follow my passions,
even when I didn't quite know myself.

I love you both.

The Waters

Page

.	In Love	1
. .	Out of Love	22
. ..	Wanting Love	54
∴	In Faith	68
. ∴	Separation	84
:::	Friends	97
:: .. .	Family	111
:: ::	Addiction	120
:::: .	Life & Self	126
:.: :.:	The World	150

Acknowledgements

Although many of these poems were written long before my spiritual journey was becoming clearer to me, I would be sadly amiss in not acknowledging all my family, friends, mentors, teachers and clergy along the path who have touched and enriched my life with their love, warmth, forgiveness and insight.

I also acknowledge the impact of the teachings and inspiration of Bruce Lee, Jiddu Krishnamurti, Alan Watts, Shunryū Suzuki, Neale Donald Walsch, Helen Schucman, Bill Thetford, Eva Pierrakos, Sarah Chambers, and Rupert Spira. Thank you for your willingness and dedication in paving the paths many of us walk on with flowers of guidance of highest truth and wisdom.

And to those pesky seagulls at Robert Moses State Park, whom I happily share their beach and companionship with during occasional walks in the quiet of nature—and to my parents who encouraged such walks in the evening for many years—see you soon.

Foreword

Finding poetry that resonates with me can be challenging.

Often, it's hit-or-miss, and I know rather quickly if the relationship is going to work. So, I'd like to thank you for spending your time in trying to form a relationship with me through this, my first work.

This collection contains poems written throughout my life, while unknowingly navigating a path of self-growth through increasing self-awareness. Upon returning to these poems decades later, I noticed the topics fell naturally into groupings which captured various aspects of our Unity, ever-present within our finite individual subjective experiences of objective reality. While these poems have been inspired by my own experiences, my hope is they express emotions which resonate with you on your journey, giving you some warmth and new insight. If this occurs, then I believe this book was meant to find you.

The journey continues. Living waters flow and create anew. I am grateful for this chance to share my life with you, to remain open to recognizing my own false, static ideas about life where I may have covered them over, and to experiencing anew the sensations of the heart, the body and the world as manifestations of our Unity.

Enjoy reading! I wish you well on your journey, and I hope something shared within can make lighter, clearer, more transparent, whatever you may be carrying with you, possibly unknowingly.

In Unity,
Kevin Haszto, 2019

In Love

◆

About You

So, I just want to know
Do you want to go out?
Do you want to paint the town red and white tonight?

So, I just want to know
Are you sick of all those games?
Are you looking for a change in your life tonight?

Well, I see what's in your heart
And I swear it's in mine too
And I care too much about it, too much about you

Gratitude Song

And so it is already to me
And will continue to be
As we grow older together
It was always meant to be
And I could always see that
In your eyes

It's gratitude I hold in the well of my heart
It's joy that I feel in my soul from the start
Even when we're crying or just torn up inside

It's gratitude I hold in the well of my heart
It's joy that I feel in my soul from the start
It's your arms I run to, even when I want to hide

I Love You

Running around, looking for a place that is my own
Running away, looking for time all alone
Hiding from the past: it's not so far behind
Looking for an answer, scared to know what I'll find

Running around, looking for that place, yours to own
Running away, looking for the hand to guide me home
Scared about the future: it's not so far ahead
Closing my eyes so tight, where will I be led?
And I find you
You were there to pull me through
And I found you

Running in circles I keep meeting you again
Never a thought, distrust, never thinking this "the end"
But only the means, the way, to some greater reason why
Don't know why that I didn't see I'd never say goodbye
To you
You are here to pull me through
And I love you

And I found you
You are here to pull me through
I never lost my faith in you
And now I'm here to pull you through
And I love you

Always with Me

I arrived in your life
You needing me most
I would've come sooner

My calling of your name
Unlikely it seemed
Was always devoted to you

More than I ever knew
More than we ever hoped
Already intertwined

Your garden is planted
You're never far from my heart
You're always with me

Speechless

Your smile, your eyes
Your just saying, "Hi"
You make me speechless every time

Your style, your way
Your interest today
You make me speechless everyday

Just about every time you walk into the room
Just as you walk on by wearing sweet perfume
Just about every way you seem to look at me
You make me speechless
I know you want me

Temper Me

Temper that pleasure with some bittersweet pain
Temper that love with a small dose of fear
Temper that kiss with a little confusion
And you have us

Temper that filling with a bit of active void
Temper that quenching with a little blazing fire
Temper that lick with a little scratch
And you have us

Temper that learning with some lingering doubt
Temper that living with thoughts of left behind
Temper that contentment with a bit of passion
And you have us

But you can't change the presence that we have
And you cannot live another day
Knowing that we aren't because we are
And what you have when all is left is undeniably us

Just be certain that I always
Temper your distance with your constant presence
Temper this confusion with my love for you always
Temper this time being split in two with a union that makes me whole

And in my heart, it lingers so
What you have when everything is left behind
When everything is let go
When there is nothing else to live for is us

Temper me with a little bit of you
And what we have is us

The Road to Return

I see a road, you are there too
And seldom has it been traveled
And only by few
I see a way, it leads through you
It may not always be easy
But we will get through

You're not wrong to feel what you feel in this moment
And I'm not wrong to feel what it is that I do
But I know there's a way that we will keep it together
And see each other through

It may take some listening to things
We don't particularly enjoy
Remembering that they are calls for love
It may take some ceiling gazing or some time away
To gather our thoughts and our will to go on
But we'll remember we cannot be deprived
Of anything except by our own hand

Carefree

Ever since I met you it's only grown
The smile in my mind, the face your own
The time it takes inside for me to see
That it felt so right, you close to me
And looking in your eyes it's carefree

And while we both sit here wondering
With me holding on to your everything
You lean back inside my being
And just forget any bad feeling
And resting in your arms it's carefree

The Best That I Can

Many times, I've prayed for someone special
For them to come along
But as I sat there and prayed
I was just singing my sad songs
Now I have to get up
And take this chance
And change my life again
So, I'll take command
I'll take a stand
And I'll do the best that I can

When I picked up this paper and pencil
I thought I knew what to say
But as I sat there thinking
All those words just went away
You know you mean so much to me
You know how much I care
You know if you were hurting
I'd want to be there
To comfort you with my hands
And to do the best that I can

It's so hard to open up
Since rejection hurts me so
It's a chance that I must take
I guess it's time to grow
I've not done it before
But I know I have to show
It's time to open up
It's time for me to grow

Tour Guide

Tour guide—I need a hand
Help me, I don't understand
I'm sorry, it's just who I am
Tour guide
Tour guide—my heart is weak
Hold me, don't let me speak
I'm crazy and the outlook is bleak
Tour guide

Could you show me around this world of mine?
Keep me in check, keep me in time
Find me the places to rest my soul
Take me to the water whole

Tour guide—you certified?
I hope so, because I need to hide
I said something, my foolish pride
Tour guide
Tour guide—I can't see you now
Show me where, why and how
I hurt you, I just won't allow it
Tour guide

Tour guide—don't stay away
Tomorrow's a brand-new day
Could you show me how to laugh and play?
Tour guide
Tour guide—you with me, love?
You know I'm here, if you need a hug
Because tour guides might need someone sometimes
Tour guide

Day One

There is so much I wish to say
About how wonderful you are
For me, in this or that way
And I awake this morning
A hope shining within
Only to light the room afire
Only to wake my heart
From its place of decay

I hear the "yes"
And I know where we stand
No denying the fact
I am your man
And I hope it to be
The beginning...
No, not the beginning
The most meaningful union
For you, for me

We are new people
Never the same
With new budding fruit
The season as long as the inverse of pace
And it's not a race
And however poetic it still seems to be
It's simply you
It's simply me

Where to Go from Here

We really both enjoyed ourselves
But I really don't know how
Did we do anything special
Maybe it's that we're with each other now?
It's not as if we've done things together
That would be fun just doing alone
But it is your presence, your existence I find fun

Would it be too much to say that I find you very beautiful?
That I find myself at peace whenever I'm with you?
Can I honestly say without turning back
That my heart wants more of what I lack?
And you might have it
You might own it
But my gun-shy attitude keeps coming back
And I can't help it

I come to this point and I come again
I think you're more than just a friend
I come to this point as I came before
But I'm not knocking down the door
Of tomorrow
Of the future
Of where to go from here

How, Why or What From

It's been some time, it's you and me
Amazing how this seemed meant to be
We make a new promise of what will come
We're satisfied not knowing how, why or what from

And how I'd love to hold you in my arms tonight
To silence any fear, to swim inside our light
That place is my home—it's where you are
Connections are but meetings of chance
And you grace my life from afar

That Place, Called Home

Although I don't want to see you go
I just saw a look in your eyes
Some longing for your homeland
A new chance for some goodbyes

Another heartache
Another break
Another chance that you will take
As I sorely think of saying bye
I want you to go
I wonder why

Maybe it was that glimmer in your eyes
Or just the excitement as you talked
That glint, or when you apologized
For speaking German in the back seat of the car

Somehow, I realized just how much it means to you
That place, called home

All I Own

And the normality I feel scares me
And the unity tears apart
And the parts that are left in limbo
Are stretched between our hearts
And the burden, released, envelopes
And the twist of fate arrests
And the time it takes for me to brake
Is too short even for best
And the lines that are crossed so quickly
And the intimacy that is lost
Are surely the signs, the warning signs
Of time ill-spent, embossed
On the face I bring forth with me
On the distances that we'll face
And I know this chance, this circumstance
Could easily make, break or replace
All I own

My Guitar Nearby

When I held you that night
I felt so right
We read through my lyrics, my guitar nearby
I felt so sure
Not at all insecure
But I didn't really understand why

With two common friends
Sitting far from the ends
Of their seats, both involved in our talk
You helped me to feel
That my feelings were real
Not just some "emotional walk"

So, I thanked you a lot
And you answered, "for what?"
And I said, "For all that you've done
Like sunlight to a tree
You really helped me
To open up and bask in the sun"

Now I will not forget
What you did for me and yet
I will not compete with any other man
You're so important to me
So, I hope you can see
That I just want to hold you again

When I held you that night
I felt so right
We read through my lyrics, my guitar nearby

These Memories of You

The movie playing in the other room—
The violence
Means nothing to me at all
The scent on my shirt
Because of your embrace—
Only you
Your arms I was holding onto
Matter to me

So, I lay my heart out to be slaughtered
But instead it's embraced by one so dear
The feeling I had inside meant everything to me
Right now, and right here
But I'm not hungry
And I'm fine
I'm just torn apart
Your world and mine

And so, I find

What I own here today
Is more than I ever had
Even though it's without you
You're here in my heart
I'll just make do
And stand the days
And tolerate the time
And live my life
And hold on to
These memories of you

I Tremble

I tremble when I hold you
And I can't control myself
So, security means a lot to me
And not to someone else
So, I tremble when you hold me
Though I try to be myself
But I still tremble when I hold you
So just try to be yourself

Don't close the door until we all come through
Don't close the door
Yes, I'm talking to you

I don't know what makes me feel unsafe
And I don't care anymore
But I'll just close my eyes and fly
Right through the open door

Having You

I can see myself, my happiness true
Since I know that I've loved you
I might not have you here today
But I own you in my heart and way

I see you so in all I do
That I won't say I don't have you
You've become a part of my life, so true
All's to say is, "I love you"

Two Bodies, One Spirit

You and I
On a beach
Crashing waves
Full, moonlit night
Our joined silhouettes
Back-lit by the moon
Our faces reflecting starlight
We chase moonbeams
In circles as waves crash

Summertime
We play joyfully
Gleefully within the energy
That surrounds
That fills us

Waist deep
Playful
You and I
We are joined
As we are
And as we will be
Two bodies
One spirit

Out of Love

◆ ◆

Alone

So, where are you?
You did not phone
I'm so concerned and so alone

I thought I'd be
The first one you'd call
So, I'm worried about it all

You weren't at work
Did you book a flight?
I feel alone, so I thought I'd write

I tried to call
But no one's home
I'm so concerned and so alone

The Sweetness of the Moment

That is what my life is like without you
Only searching for my life in what I can't do
I stay here all alone
Never mind what I did wrong
Somewhat happy in all that's happened
Somewhat sad in all that's not
After all of the sweetness of the moment is gone

So, I stay here cursing the day
Instead of rejoicing in the past
Thinking not of what I had
But instead of what I don't
And a year ago now comes to mind
And the time when I first called you
And all I began to own
And all that I had grown
In the light of my new-found truth
Which changed my life for years to come
But this love is now like a sour taste lingering upon my lips
Constant testimony to the sweetness I'm hoping to regain
After all of the sweetness of the moment is gone

The Bitter Pill

You've come into my world
And turned it upside down
That it's right side up again
I'm understanding what's around
But now that you're leaving again
All that which was just static
Has jostled around a little bit
And made me quite erratic

And I'm not making this
Any easier for myself
And I see this too
Not like it will affect you
There it goes, selfishness again
Your feelings still
What's in my will?
Time to take the bitter pill

Our Time Together

Do you remember the day
When our love was new
When our days were young
When I loved you?
Though our love is gone
I loved you true
I look back at us
And I only see you

My love is gone
The same old song
My heart is weak
And the doubt is strong
My love is weak
And it won't be long
Until my heart is gone
And I'm all alone

Our time together
Once seemed forever
But now it's gone

Day Two

I've hit day two
No turning back
No looking at how things were
I've hit day two
I won't look back
Although I'm not quite sure
How I will survive
And make it through
This battle between me and you

It looks like we're all waiting
And we're searching for something
Hoping for something
It seems like we're not happy where we are
It looks like we're all waiting
And we're searching for something
Hoping for something
Is there something left to satisfy our needs?

Northern Outlook

We had a moment in time
We danced sensation and bright lights
Wandered across the dark
Horizon fades away
Then it was gone
With one sunset
And I fumbled to hit rewind

I desired to relive all the hours
Our treasured memories
Though it was not meant to be
Our tortured melodies
And all controls
Control was gone
Come back to me, my love

I look into the skies for the brightest star
I know that this is where I can't find you anymore
Take me across to your new north horizon
We can't relive yesterday

Give me a chance to rediscover True North with you
We'll be showered nightly in the shared starlight
A new today
Souls intertwined
Side-by-side forever redefined

Heal Thyself

Why must I be so glued on you
And make myself so miserable?
Why must I be so glued on you
And fall over— fall over— fall over so?
And yet, I know you have to go
So why must— why must I love you so?

"For so long you've just been on your own
You've never asked, you've never grown
And now you want just some small help?"
He said, "Christian, Christian, heal thyself!"

So I See

Why is this feeling in my heart?
Why do these thoughts tear me apart?
Why can't I stop this damn barrage?
Where do I fit in this collage?
Just let me out, get it out of me!
So, I ask you
So I see

I'm too damn patient
And too damn kind
Too damn forgiving
And too damn blind
I'm too damn loving
And too damn nice
Too understanding
They're cold as ice

Why can't she call when she gets home?
Why do I feel so damn alone?
And so betrayed, it makes me feel
So, should I care if this is real?
Just let me out, get it out of me!
So, I ask you
So I see

Away

There's this sadness in my heart since you've been away
There's this emptiness of purpose each and every day
There's this crying out in silence and there's nothing left to say
I just miss you
I just miss you

There's this lack of true direction and a convincing of my heart
The mind is just so tired trying to make another start
There's this hopelessness that time will linger on until it's dead
I just miss you
I just miss you

I wish I knew just what to do to stop the pain of each heartbreak
I'll make it through this meaninglessness no matter how much longer it takes
And your happiness I hear will console my heart even as mine aches
And one day you'll never leave me again
And one day you'll never go away

Will Grow in Time

I just don't know if you will call
And I just don't know if you care at all
But from our last conversation
I could swear that our relations
Will grow in time

I hate the fact that you haven't called
And I hate the fact I don't know at all
But from this time that I'm waiting
My feelings I'm retaining
Will grow in time

I just don't care if you don't call
And I don't care if you care at all
Because my sights are now setting
A new target, I'm betting
Will grow in time

As I Am?

Now I have a woman who thinks she
Accepts me as I am!
Now I have a woman who thinks she
Accepts me as I am!

I love her
Oh, she tries
She's convinced
Controlling
She is not
But I know

She tells me how
She hates controlling women
Well, maybe I should walk outside
To find me?

Sensing but Apart

Meet me here in my own life
To lose control, to be my wife
To place myself upon your knee
To find my light in us, in we

Until I quiet my own head
I'm only feeling as good as dead
Until I see with my own heart
I'm only sensing but apart

Put Me to Bed

What suddenly changed
That you needed to chat
Not, "I have to go"
That you called me back?

What made you change
Your sulking into words
Which tried to communicate
Your bewilderment
Of others
Of life?

Keep pointing the finger
I don't have a mirror tonight
I added some small words
Then you put me to bed

My Love's Been Crucified

Is my love in vain
And if so, where's the pain?
I hope no wounds remain
But I know it won't be the same

Without you by my side
All those tears I've cried
Run like a river past my heart
Why did it hurt me inside?

I hunger more because I'm in pain
Why don't we love all the same?
It is here in this grave you lied
I feel my love's been crucified

Without You

Now that you're gone
I wonder why
We said hello to say goodbye
We said bonjour to say so long
But now it's gone
Now it's gone

I held you close for just so long
But now I sing— I sing this song
You're gone and I'm here in my life
Without you

Solace Now

So, we talked about a drive—
A ride at night
Headlights off, feeling right
So, we closed our eyes
Though we said we're blind
We didn't want to open them
To see what we'd find
Solace now

I asked you, "Am I right,
Uncovering my eyes?"
I thought it really mattered
Whether or not we saw lies
You claimed you weren't afraid
To see the life we made
But you just closed your eyes
And slowly but surely faded into
Solace now

Ignorance is bliss
But it's sad that you'll miss
All the wonders of this world
All the life
You might be happy there
Fleeing to your rocking chair
Wanting solace now
To be your knife

Who Could Ask for More?

You counted to three and never made the bed
And always made breakfast but only in your head
Inspiring my world, my one white dove
Flying over the oceans and leaving me to love

I counted to ten and always made the bed
And never made breakfast but only in your head
I was your taproot brother, your life having begun
You were my watering mother, it left you to run

Finding you impulsive, never happy, immature
I ask you, who could ask for more?

Now we count to two thousand and don't share the same bed
And we'll never share breakfast, we are only in my head
Never felt so lonely, a full moon in the sky
Felt as my devil below and my angel on high

Finding me devoted but overbearing for sure
I ask you, who could ask for more?

Now I count your letters on one hand
You have the countless sum of mine?
I was the chair on which you stood to grab
Your nourishment, air and wine
But when you spread your wings to fly away
I was left the only one
Overshadowing the moon in a blazing sky
And you outshining the sun

In Duress

It's hard to live without you
Day by day here by my side
And challenges within our lives
Make our chances pass us by

To say I miss you
Is not enough to express
The longing within my heart for you
And so, for now, we're in duress

What Senselessness Is

I guess you'll never understand
What my bridge I built has crossed
I guess you'll stay ignorant to
My feelings that you've tossed

Old proverbs are now dying
As I long to hear cliché again
And old times lie sadly still
And buried for years
And it's no use trying
To dig up their bones

They've sunken down into the pile of piles
Beneath shovel loads of angst—miles and miles
I can't care what separates me from them
I can't bear to see why, how, and when
And I'm so tired of sensing
What senselessness is

This

I just don't know anymore
Is it anger or just confusion
That I couldn't say these words to you?
And now that I can you're across the Atlantic
While I sit here speaking in my own sort of tongues
Writing you all that's in my heart
Until there's no more left

And all that's left is what inevitably rises out of the ashes
Of burnt emotions once intensely burning
But now smoldering and consuming my life
By how it changes my view of this world

How it marks my spirit
I can't put you away, I can't leave you behind
In my heart it's anger I find
That this could occur, and I must learn to deal
With just how real this is

For just about eight letters
I only wrote on the pages you saw
I couldn't express any more, nor did I want to
Since all that I needed, all that I wanted
Was to be still part of your life

Though you were away
I could only pray
For your constant contact in any form
From you to me
There could only be
One way this was—a soliloquy
And I still learned to deal
With just how real this was

And now there's so much more
That I can't write you in a letter
Now I just can't express
These feelings to you
They began to arise
Only after your leaving
Only after my heart began to scream
And bleed from its shell
While returning to your home
You began to confide
In my trust and my world
Not making it any easier
For me to let go

But understand
I love you
And if I knew you needed me
To be there with you
Or anywhere
I would be there
Even though I don't know
How to deal
With just how real this is

Freedom and Indifference

So, what if this matters to me
And what if you don't really care?
And what role am I to play
Me over here, you over there?

Our views can't survive in a vacuum
Our lives can't grow on their own
Our voices will just fade away as we both sit here at home
Both together, both alone, yet most alone

Only down the road when we looked back
We saw what our lives had become
Did we understand, but failed to plan
What could happen when you love someone?

We planned to find before our lives entwined
What to do, where to go, how to live
But we committed too fast and thought it'd last
I have no more blood left to give

So, I thought I would give you something new
I give you the freedom so you can choose
The life we led was quite possibly our best
But autonomy and apathy were better than the rest
Yes, freedom and indifference were our very best

What I Won't Do

I'm sitting here listening to my song for you
Looking at your picture knowing what I can't do

I'm sitting here thinking of all the things that could've been
And all the things which pull me through

I'm crying in my mind a thousand tears
Until on the earth there is no land
But I feel as if I did that too
You would not understand
Just how much you mean to me
Just how much I would do
Just how much I could not live
Tomorrow without you

I'm sitting here looking at your picture
Knowing what I won't do

Whatever You Might Think

I don't just want this relationship
Because it is convenient
Though I do want to grow old
With someone and have someone to love
Whatever you might think
I still love you
And it's hard for you to own up to it
Whatever I might think
You still know it
Though it's hard for me to show it
And it's not for us to grow it
We cannot change the people that we are

The Letting Go of All That I Know

Why does it have to be
Such a beautiful day today?
Why is it when things go wrong
You just cannot be sad at all?
Why do You cheer me up so much?
Why do You hold me up?
Why don't You let me fall?

So now I'm demanding
Retribution as to what
Got me into this mess
And initially made the cut
And still You cheer me up so much
And still You hold me up
Why don't You let me go?

Clouds are leaving, the rain is gone
Off from work, Monday morn
Taking care of problems still
But I just can't see past this hill

The answer, it seems
Lies within the letting go
Of her, of me, of all that I know

Painstaking, Still Questioned

I wonder why I let you do this, on and on, to me
And God helps out in this for my confusion to grow
It's His tool in all this, painstaking, still questioned
My love for you is true though

And I sit on the phone, the call
Only occurring because of how much I care
And how I cannot kick out the wounded puppy
It's the tears and bruises of the dog that bit my leg
That's painstaking, still questioned
My love for you is true though

You clearly made it known I shouldn't
Why do I continue to love one so beaten?
Either respect your opinion and feel divided in this
Or recognize the opposition that's painstaking, still questioned
My love for you is true though

The way you answer me
Makes me out to be some S.O.B.
That couldn't give a damn about how you feel
And what you endure, yes, that's painstaking, still questioned
My love for you is true though

Near leaving, worth trying
Under the flat that's worn into the rim
Clearly beaten, or was that a whip I heard?
Whichever way, it's painstaking, still questioned
My love for you is true

Back for More

In the past it was so much easier
To dismiss what I saw circling before my eyes
But now all I seem to notice
Is this surreal possibility
And my heart is making me cry
And when I don't know the truth
It presents itself on the page

Why must I come back for more?
Why must I lie down on the floor?
God help myself where I lie
The time is gone when I once could say goodbye
and I'm back again, I'm here again
I won't let you take control
But God knows, I can't let go!

In my life it became evident
That I could break the chains
Surrounding me everyday
But now they're back
And I cannot see it any other way
And when I know the truth
My hands are tied with lies

How can I refuse to be myself?
God please help those who won't help themselves
Why bless these people with forgiving hearts?
Because the time is back and I can't stand to part
And I'm back again, I'm here again
I won't let you take control
But God knows, I can't let go!

1 to 2

She is everything to me
She is happiness to be
She is pleasurable by far
She is all I ever want
She is time and time again
She is clearly my best friend
But all I ever do is try
To justify, to ask me why

There is nothing here for me
There's no happiness to be
There's no pleasure here by far
Just be alone is all I want
Seeing time and time again
To see it's easier to end
So why have I tried and tried
To keep it alive?

Wayside

I have much more self-respect
Than to let this bother me
Than to let you hurt me
Than to go on like this
This way

I have much more insight
Than to let you make me believe
That you want to continue
On this way

I own much more in my heart
Than you could ever know
And so, with you by my wayside
I've grown

Changes

It's already faded
It's almost gone
And all I have left is that same old song
My interest ebbs
And my feelings change
As the photos I have just rearrange

I can't deny myself at all
Forever is too strong for me
I cannot say that I'm in love
Because then I would be lying to thee

It's already faded
It's almost gone
The notes now, somehow, just seem so wrong
My interest wanes
And my feelings change
As I start to see I don't feel the same

Letters from Holland

I think I see a reason of this leaving me behind
I think I see some benefits I've gotten out this time
But the freedom I've got inside of me
Can only— can only set me free
While security, it feeds
By letters from Holland
To me

I know I see a reason this time
I know I see a reason and I'm making up my mind
Oh, the freedom I've got inside of me
Can only— can only set me free
While security, it feeds
By letters from Holland
To me

Wanting Love

It Must Be You

And it isn't enough that I'm already disabled
In making my feelings known
We must now be encumbered by the tower of babel
No chance for you to be shown

And it isn't enough to say that I'll miss you
Not understanding just how it's meant
And it's just too damn much to say, "I love you"
Letting all my emotions vent

Just how I feel, it is so real
Spinning round and round the language wheel

So, I just have to say it, in a way, explain it
That you see it, it is so true
So, I just have to say, "To spend every day
with someone, it must be you"

Today with You

And so, I am sitting here
On my bed
Looking at my pencil
And eraser
Just thinking about you

Ready for bed
Ready to dream
Just thinking about
How bright you shine
Just thinking about you in time

In someone else's life
Someone else's dream
Someone else's time
How bright you'll shine
Just thinking about you

And maybe I'll start thinking
About you here in my life
About you here in my sky
Shining bright and I'll have you
Just thinking about us in time

This moment is still here
I'll only lose it with my fear
And so, I am sitting here
On my bed
Just thinking about you

Hollow

So many poems about love
In the languages of the heart
With words the intellect finds dull
But somehow the simple reigns
And the common becomes sublime
Although, no challenge to the mind
But instead they might free our soul
Emotions on a single page
Somehow reflect all that is
All that was or will be
And all that matters

And all we long for is
Some true companion
Some friend, some lover
Who will never let us down
And can identify with us
In the midst of our troubles
Some turn to the page
And for some it's the only one there
To help cope with their trouble

Or rejoice in delight
Or feel their pain
This endless emptiness
That emotion creates
Within the soul of one
Whose happiness
Is in question
And so, what is static, sustains
And in this hollow we are whole

No One Knows

No one knows when it could come
When love could come into your life

I just didn't know
It happened so fast
I prayed to God that it could last
I just didn't know
It happened so fast

Right about that time
Of least hope and most despair
She was there

All the Rest

I know you're out there somewhere
And I will meet you then
But I haven't found out where just yet
And I haven't found out when
All I've seen so far in life
Are just faint copies at best
But I think it might be you
You're not like all the rest

You're just someone
In my dreams, in my mind
In my life, I hope I find
Someone like you, I think I know
I hope I see where to go
To find you there
But understand
I go nowhere

Plow through Time

Plow through time
Yours and my time
Plow through time
So, we could be together

Leave the Romance

Maybe I should leave the romance
To the ones who have no trouble expressing themselves
To the ones who don't need paper and pencil to feel free
But my heart longs for someone to love
And I ask for a reason to live
But I can't find another

Insecurity

Not ready to make a commitment
Not ready to go on a date
Not ready to go steady
Just wondering about my fate
Not ready for what I want, yeah
Not ready to get intense
I'm not ready to move a little closer
I'm just ready to sit on the fence

Not ready to show it all
Not ready to make things real
Not ready to act on love
Can't tell you how I feel
I'm not ready to open up
I'm not ready to bear it all
Not ready to stand up straight
I'm just worried, lest I fall

I'm not ready to take off my mask
Not ready to show my face
I'm not ready to feel vulnerable
Not ready, this time, this place
I guess I am so insecure
I'm not ready to be on the brink
I really have to stop wondering
About what everyone else thinks

April Fool

Hello, here I am just for you, acting cool
Because I am an April fool
Hello, here I am again, eyes are truly glued on you
Because I am an April fool
Hello, here I am, staring blatantly so true at you
Because I am an April fool
Hello, here I am again, hiding again from you
Always going to be an April fool

Flowers blooming, getting warm
My heart is yet always torn
And what I see and what I feel
My foolishness is always real
It's no big deal

Stay (This Memory)

So, I just don't know how three days ago
I saw your face but now I can't place
So, I just want time to stay quite still
For this momentary indecision in
Your look, your eyes, your way
I ask this memory to stay

To look into your eyes
And find a chance of my happiness
As a rose is accepted and held near
How I'd like to remember you, dear
Can I renew my picture
With these feelings that I own?
Can I embrace this love and see
Your look, your eyes, your way?
I ask this memory to stay

Her

Now that I remember her face
I'm happier every day
Now that I've visited the place
I see the hope which lights my way

I'd love to see her, to be with her
And to hold her and to fear her
I'd love to touch her and to love her
To respect her and be near her

But alas, I don't know you all that well
And I know and I see that the future
Is just something that I can't tell

Closer to Me

The longing in my heart is not satisfied
The thoughts within my mind draw me near
Closer to the page where I lay down my life
Closer to the heart, closer, I fear

So tonight, I lay my thoughts down
And these words here on the page draw me near
Closer to the time when I lay it on the line
Closer to the heart, closer, I fear

So sometimes I'm not looking but just in my mind I see
You close to me
Closer to me

But sometimes I am looking and within my mind I see
You close to me
Closer to me

On My Mind

The phone does ring at eight o'clock as I am writing songs
I jump up fast and hope and pray as seconds last so long
I question who is on the phone because I hope it's you
It's not, I sigh, and say goodbye and hope that you get through

The phone again at nine o'clock rings over in my head
I run and leap and nearly drop to answer it instead
I jump up fast and hope and pray as seconds last so long
But since it wasn't you that called, I'm back to writing songs

You're on my mind so much today that I just had to call
I can't stop thinking about us both, I just can't stop at all
It's the Lord, you know, He spins me around and makes me wonder still
About the path down which I walk, about the milk I spill

So, I decide
Not to hide

In Faith

The Burdens We Share

We all have our burdens
And we all have our deaths
We all have our goodbyes
And we don't know what's left

We all will be learning that
We all have each other
And we just might understand
The whole world is our brother

In the burdens we share

Treasures

What I know now is not a lot
Later it will be complete
As well as You know me now
My love for You will never deplete

FAITH is following You to the end
Thank God I found You in my heart
When I touch my hands, I see Your face
More perfectly than ever before

HOPE is knowing You're always there
My new life awaits Your every word
Light shines brighter in the darkness
My eyes to Your visage would make me blind

LOVE is keeping a warm place in Your heart
Knowing You'll be there with me
During hard times You give me strength
Patiently I await Your every word

Throughout this tribulation
All but three precious things will die
If anything should ever come down from above
The greatest of all these gifts is LOVE

Yesterday Again

Slam the bit within the mouth of freedom
Fly, fly, upward fly
Kill the anger of your forty-second scream down
"Why?" I ask you, "Why?"
Stab the want of killing, closer, ever closer, and then
Gladly, hold the energy in your hands

Play within the day of life unfolding
And care, and love, and then
Draw ever closer to the time you're holding
Onto dearly, slipping, nearly gone
And keep, and climb, and stay a while
And love, and hold the peace in your hands

Judas Love

It's profound, not profane
It's around but not mundane
Into law, traveling crime
Passing from common to sublime

Love one another, yes, each other
Enemies as well as friends
Love one another, brother-to-brother
Now's the time to let Him mend our hearts

Judas love is on the outside, real love on the in
Receiving Love right now is where to begin

Trust in Him

And Love will do, whatever we ask in Love's name
And Love will do, whatever we ask in Love's name
And Love said, "I will do, whatever you ask
In My name, whatever you ask"
and Love said, "I will do, whatever you ask
In My name"

He didn't tell us to reach for the stars
He only told us to trust in Him
He didn't tell us to try to win the race by ourselves
He only told us to trust in Him

In the name of Love
Love will do

The Transfiguration

After six days, Jesus took Peter, James, and John
And led them up a high mountain where they were all alone
There he was transfigured before them
His face shone like the sun
And his clothes became as white as the light

And there appeared Moses and Elijah
Peter said, "Rabbi, it is good to be here
Let us erect three booths—one for You
One for Moses, and one for Elijah too!"

A Voice came from the cloud which enveloped them
"This is My Son, whom I love, listen to Him!"
Suddenly, when they looked all around and were shocked
There was no light at all, in fact, it was very dark

How sometimes I wish, sitting in my room
Singing with guitar to some same old tune
That I could be there with all my heart
Then I realize He's as bright as light from the very start
And all I have to do is look inside my heart

To Meet with You

A rainy morn, a sunny afternoon
Refreshing dawn, the darkest night
Until the morn
LOVE's circle slides me to meet with You

A run through Your amusement park
Slid through the night, left me in the dark
Light the spark
FAITH's circle slides me to meet with You

Saturday, just a day away
Run through the night, one moment away
Can I stay?
HOPE's circle slides me to meet with You

So real in my life
To touch one's soul so close
So revealing, so everlasting
So real, so true, so close

The New Birth of Tomorrow

No matter how much I seem to run away
I always find You there
No matter how many times I want to cry
You always dry my tears

No matter how many times I curse the day
You always seem to show me
What the new birth of tomorrow might bring

Walk by Faith

The word is near you, in your mouth and your heart
Just as we are one member of the body one part
With your mouth you confess and your heart you believe
In this hope we are saved for this hope is not seen

Life is close now and soon you'll see
You can lay all your burdens at His feet
Ever since I found out about His grace
I don't ever want to go back to that place

Life is close now and soon you'll see
You can lay all your burdens at His feet
Although I still have troubles and I know I have my doubts
He's there to spark my spirit when my fire's out

For we walk by faith and not by sight
We live by prayer, not by might
We live in Love, we walk in light
We walk by faith, not by sight

Place

You see, I have a place that I can go
It's a hiding place from all my foes
It is my Home

You know, I could not stand a single day
If underneath I thought You would not stay
In my Home

You know, I would not last another day
If underneath I thought that You would stray
From my Home

I meet You there in my hiding place
And I feel so alive when I see Your face
And I know You won't leave without a trace
Not alone
My Home

Talk with God

I just had the best talk with You
Some may not truly understand
At times I sighed, at times I cried
And it was not just me babbling aloud again
You talked to me

And so, for tonight, I'll not stray from Love
And not due to some form of punishment
But instead, because I just don't want to—
It hurts me when I'm away
And I let You go

Now, good intentionality paves more my road
And while I may go back to negating my light
I hunger for truth and I cry more for health
And I long for Love, no matter what I may say
No matter what I might do

Learning to Walk

When I was young, He did it all
My Father in heaven wouldn't let me fall
He helped me to walk and I was so proud
Not falling, just walking, upon a soft cloud

How sure I was then when I was so young
Every time that I prayed an answer would come
But then as I grew God expected some more
So sometimes I'd trip and fall on the floor

When not understanding, I questioned the Lord
"Where did you go? Who cut the cord?"
But lately I realize the Lord didn't go
And He's still my guide as I learn to grow

I'm learning to walk

Renewal

I'm wandering the street alone at night
With separation to feed
All alone, I lost my fight
I don't know what my spirit needs
It's a seed with no apparent growth
For the last sixteen years
The only warmth is from my coat
That is stained by my recent tears

Life's without hope, world's full of sin
I know what I did is somehow wrong
I'm always searching my heart for a new life to begin
I let Your Spirit speak its unified song
I cry out in the night, "Jesus, where are you?"
I cry out again and again
Into my heart Your Spirit flew
And helped me by moving within

I turned my eyes to You
You lifted me up to your side
No slave to fear whenever You're near
I have no reason to hide
You washed me whiter than snow
You saved one lost like me
Grasping for no thing in my heart
In no time You set me free

By His Wounds

Surely, He took up our infirmities
And carried our sorrows
Yet we considered Him stricken by God
Smitten by Him and afflicted
But He was pierced for our transgressions
He was crushed for our iniquities
The punishment that brought us peace was upon Him
And by His wounds
We are healed

All My Songs

Thank you, Lord, for helping me
Through these last two months I see
That You have given me a peace of mind
A salvation above any kind

I'm so glad to know as the storm disappears
As the desert land ends, as the water draws near
You've been standing beside me all along
And You've guided me through all my songs

Oh Father, I know I am your son
We all keep fighting but I know You've won
You've paid the price and filled my bones
So now I know what I've always known: I'm not alone

No matter how long the desert land lasts
Or the storm's around before it's passed
When I felt like I was all alone
You held my hand through all my songs

Separation

My Soul

Jesus, I am back
I hope you haven't gotten lonely
Without me standing firmly
Oh, so firmly on your word
Jesus, I am here
And although I could be much closer
To you, closer, so much closer
I am not, I know, I fear

So please Lord, lift me up
Back to the level of Your grace
To see the beauty of Your face
I would ask it be my place
So please Lord, lift me up
Restore the ashes of my soul
Please gather up and make me whole
For life has taken its fair toll
On me, my soul

Go with Me

There's a battle coming up, Lord
Please, go with me
There's an attack on my soul
Please, go with me
There's a vantage point to which I
Please, go with me
I cannot control
Please, go with me
Into this endless winter night

I don't want to disappear
Into this endless winter night
Into what I see upcoming
Without putting up a fight

No silent Spring will hold me
No vantage point control me
I'm hanging on this thread
Because of what You told me
Because of what You said

A New Beginning / Just a Stone's Throw Away

A flower blooming, a new born morning
A seed that's died now lives again
A new beginning, the old death dies
"You will find your heart where your treasure lies"

As sand in the hourglass scatters as it cracks
So, my life lies dormant, scattered artifacts
My old friends are now back for the attack
All the treasure in the world just distracts
From my new beginning

Whatever I do
Wherever I go
I see You there

Rose in the desert, cry from the heat
Just a stone's throw away from my wandering feet
Living time's edge lies straight ahead
Moving speed's line, I'm being led
I will see You face-to-face

I can't believe it's true
How am I there for You?
I really don't know what to say
I'm just a stone's throw away

About It

The only reason I ask you
About the weather
Is I am bored
And I don't care about it
Anymore
I see a little problem
That's hidden in my plan
As I see those holy nail scars
Embroidered on Your hands
And I'm just praying
My life will change
According to Your plan
I need to see
Those holy nail scars
I need to see
What's in it for me
I need to hold it in my hand
Hold it close, so close
And I will pray to Thee
The only reason I ask you
About the weather
Is I am bored
And I don't care about it
Anymore

Strength Perfected

Your despair
And you're upset
And you fear for your kids

You want to tear down
The foundations of this life
That you live

In your weakness is My strength perfected
In your hopelessness you can count on Me
In Me you may not be able to see yourself right now
But one day you will know Us to be One

I love you

Talk to You

No feeling expressed
No expression real true
When I'm not
Talking to You

If I express
Your word will stand true
You'll speak to me
If I talk to You

When the blind lead the blind
I just don't see
Who I'll find
And who'll find me
You know, it's a crime
To be left all alone
Jesus, please help me find
My way back home

Waiting for You

I really don't mind waiting
For my car or for a light
For a cab or for a date
For a girl, always late
And I really don't mind waiting
Watch the clock, it's time to stop
And I really don't mind waiting
As long as I am with You

But weeks and months and years could go by
When I just don't understand Your plan
And time after time, I want to cry
Not knowing why it goes on and on

I really don't mind waiting
For a cab or for a date
For my car or for a light
For a girl, always late
And I really don't mind waiting
Watch my watch, it's time to stop
But I really mind waiting
When I'm waiting for You

The longing, the wanting an answer
The hurting, the wanting to know
The time, the care, oh is it there?
Not knowing why it goes on and on

Quo Vadis

So, where are you going and when will you go
So, why must you leave and how can you show
The world isn't waiting for me or for you
Quo vadis, Christ Jesus?
I do what I do

So, what if I'm wrong, I want you to stay
I only want life to continue this way
So, what if I care too much to let go
Quo vadis, Christ Jesus?
I just want to know

Test of Time

I'm just trying to open my heart
You know that it could tear me apart
I'll put my hand in Your hand
You'll make me understand
That through my darkness and crime
You'll stand, I'll stand, we'll stand the test of time

Sliding
Past an answer that eludes me
Writing
All I'm sure of, all I see
Throwing
The stone that I held onto
Reading
Nothing much appeals to me

Searching
For an answer I am sure of
Running
To the end that I can see
Trying
To watch for pitfalls, reach the mountains
Flying
With the truth that sets me free

The Sword of the Lamb

Despair seems to grip my soul
As my friends turn against me, yes, my family too
But whatever it seems, it's in-between
I know that I'll have you

Rejoicing seems so far from me
I gave them your word, they hated me
I gave them your love as best I could
But the doubts in mind, the arguments I find
Are still waiting for me

I know I'm growing but where am I going?
Why, new confusion in my life?
You consecrated me and gave me liberty
By means of Your word

Are we living lies?

Caught between the silence and the words we all say
Caught between our thoughts and the words we all pray
Caught between the building and the faith in our hearts
We're called to love one another not rip each other apart

Caught between emotion and our analytical minds
Caught between the left and right, riding the narrow line
Caught between the building and the faith in our hearts
You didn't come to bring peace but a sword that cut us apart

Let Me Know

Give me life, give me peace
Here are my loads, I need release
My shell was thick, my body numb
I wandered home, my day was done

The homeless out, the side of streets
They have more life beneath their feet
I claim this is not my problem now
I'm homeless too, no heart, no how

There is no trend, there is no way
To know why You will change my day
You love me so, I know it now
And I've become a saint somehow

Even with sin inside my bones
You didn't leave me here alone
You bless me so from day to day
I won't go back, no how, no way

So, let me know
You have a reason for this season
So, let me know
You have a season for my song

So, the devil tries to bring me down again
Blinding my eyes to the cost of my sin

I Evade, I Discover

The last couple years
I was running away from You
But now it's so clear
I was running into You

I found You there
I turned around
And ran away for the world
Many places I found
You weren't around
But there was one more place
Wait
"You're not supposed to be here!"

I wouldn't tell anyone else
No one else about this end
About this place that I arrived
Not once my closest friends

But while running away
You found me a place
To rest my head
And You gave me
Someone to turn to
In my hour of need

Friends

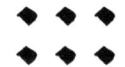

At Ease

Maybe an "oh," a "yeah," a peaceful sigh
Maybe a "szia"—the way you say goodbye
And what's the point?
Well, spending time with you places me
At ease with pieces of me

Thank you, my friend, you make life worth living
You're not the only answer—but you're the answer worth giving
At this time, this place I sip my tea
And I look all around me
I am so glad God led you to me

About Me

I open the door, you come inside
You ask the questions about what I hide
But it's not your right to what or where
It's not your right because you don't care

You wonder why but I don't care
Inside I hide, you think you're there
To question me, to think I share
Your views in life but you don't care
About me

About us
About me

So, you could call and ask and ask
But you'll just be on the outside of my life, my world

Interest

Why haven't you called back yet?
Last time we talked you said you would
Why haven't I heard from you?
I guess some things always ring true

Like you're really busy and don't have the time
If you thought me important, the time you could find
Like you figured I'd call, thus persistence again
But how many times you want my blood, one more, five, or ten?

Like with all the excuses that you could now test
It all leads back to if you have the interest

So, if I don't wait by the phone, please forgive me
So, if I wait here all alone, and I can't see
I only practice the golden rule
You know, I could be a fool

Like with all the excuses that you could now test
It all leads back to if you have the interest

My World

Do I mean to you as much as you mean to me?
Is this a one-sided friendship? Or can't I see
That I have this problem with emotions
I have so many, yes, so plenty
I'm deficient in relationships
I'm polarized again

I ask myself why I feel this way
I see myself struggling again

I want myself to be free once more
The time has come like days before
The time has come to open up
Ripe like days before
The time has come again
To desensitize my world
Unploarize my world
Uncivilize my world
Just criticized, my world

Do I mean to you
As much as you mean to me?

You're My Friend

I know you're my friend
There's something I want to tell you
The cost comes at the end
And there's something we can do

I know you're my friend
And sometimes I'd wish you'd see
The rules you can't bend
On this earth there's more than you and me

I know you're my friend
Please open your heart to me
The spirit can be mend
And all our brothers hold the key

And in my prayers, I pray for you
And I know when you pray, you pray for me too

Your soul is hurting bad
It's burning like a flame
Time to put out the fire
I know it's time Love came
Into our lives

A Midnight Clear

Christ knows where you are, knows where you're going
Knows where you were, and that you're throwing
Your voice across the room
Your life out the door living out of tune
The way your shadow moves across the shade
Your wings that fly you through the days
Proud to be who and what you are—proud to be you
It's alright, I can sympathize, but do we care? Do we hear?
The weight of the world may lie in your hands
But can we empathize on a midnight clear?

Christ knows where you are, knows where you're going
Knows where you were, and that you're growing
While playing the game it may be fun but hard to know
What road to take, which way to go
The way your light moves across the sun
Your feet that walk you to your love
Proud to be who and what you are—proud to be you
It's alright, I can sympathize, but do we care? Do we hear?
You know, I may not understand
But I love you dear on our midnight clear

Sincerely, Your Friend

Sometimes, I pray to heal my wounds
To forget troubles time didn't heal
To recall moments of glory
Forget moments of pain
Inside, I don't feel the same
Loyalties I've been running from
Like a patchwork quilt of all my friends
Influences held together by love's own pen
Knowing I should quit while I'm ahead!

A fly caught, a spider's web
My own desires drive me mad
My soul and spirit within the fire
Of peace that I once had
The freedom I had has now disappeared
The wall has been built—been built again
How quickly my actions have followed me back
Knowing I should quit while I'm ahead!

The clock on the wall might just tick away
But today just feels like yesterday

So how long has it been since we were talking on the phone?
And why was contact broken leaving us both all alone?
I missed you so—so glad to know that we're back again
So long the wait as we tempted fate—
Sincerely, your friend

Blue Cross, Silver Chain

It's funny as I look back and see the Lord's hand
Involved in every move I've made
Certain parts of life, amazing how it seems
So different to me now
And I saw the chain around your neck
And cross upon your chest
And I could not help but see
That my life has led to be
A different place again
A blue cross, a silver chain

So, if you're feeling down, my friend
Now, don't go just yet
You've got this life to live and gift to give
So, if you ever feel that He's not there
I assure you He's there and patient with us
In His own time, in His own way
For me, a blue cross, a silver chain

Emotions That We Hold

Making sure it's not a phase
Is very hard to do these days
She said—

"I wonder if you write like me
If your poems reveal your soul?
If you write about yourself to free
The emotions that you hold?
I thought that no one else but me
Could understand myself
Most people don't see past
The surface, to my inner self
The melancholy words I write
Baffle everyone else, so
It's invaluable when you can see
How much this means to me"

Needs

Why do I see the other side more often than the light?
You know I am emotional and that's not wrong or right!
You know that there's two people who I have to answer to!
So, don't condemn me now for not feeling like you do!

First is fact, then faith, and then my feelings come along
So, don't you get so damn concerned about what I write in songs!
What I need is love that adds compassion in it too
What I don't need now are more questions from you

I know what I know!
And I know how I feel!
And I know who I am!
And I know what's for real!

I Don't Need

I don't need to be under your scrutiny
Of your cold eye, of your stare
In your conviction, your condemnation of me

I don't need to see your holy judgment of me
In your glory and light don't talk down to me
Just don't try to make me see

Now, I love Christ, and I love you
But don't pawn away your savior
No matter what I do

Now, I love Christ, and I love you
But don't give me your savior
No matter what I do

Taking the Turn

So, I hate to hear it again
You know you think that I'm so wrong
Are you coming back for me?
Or is it just to make you strong?
I'm taking the turn

So, you claim to be a friend
Though you want to fence me in
When I see you, I don't want to talk
Cause there's no way that I can win
I'm taking the turn

So, my life is growing strong
And you want to hold me back
I know that you're so afraid
Of what I have and what you lack
I'm taking the turn

Until We Meet Again

Hello again, I'm here again, I'm free again
Hello again, I'm safe again, I'm near again
So, you know I love the way that I feel today
I only wish that every day could be this way
But goodbye again, until we meet again

Hello again, I'm here again, I'm free again
Hello again, I'm safe again, I'm near again
I only revel in today and pray it lasts so long
I only wish that every song could be this song
But goodbye again, until we meet again

Family

All the Same

So why are you so afraid?
Going to chase the world away?
From your children every day?
You'll shelter and protect?
Thus, suspicious and suspect?
Try to keep your kids separate?

So why are you so afraid?
The battle is what you've made
By suspicion on that fine day
So, you'll chase the world away?
But it can't ever work that way
You're simply pushing your children away

And so, it's time for them to grow up
And say goodbye to your game
The day has come for them to choose
And you will lose
All the same

Hurt

So, I take care of them all, that's where it all goes
Got twenty-four coming up, got only one thing to show
So, I ask You, I ask You so I can know

There's a man that I know who just turned twenty-one
He seems to care so much for me, my problems won't make him run
So, I ask You, I ask You so I can learn

Got into a fight with my dad last night who smacked me across my face
My esteem is low, the man I know said, "hitting your daughter's disgrace"
So, I ask You, I ask You to find my place

Why's my mother dying?
Why's my father crying?
Why does it fall upon me?
I guess I'm just called to be
The person that must hold us all together
The person torn apart
The person that has a kind heart

Jesus, Tell Me Where

It's just about that time again
And I don't seem to care
It's time to take abuse from them
It's what I hate
And it's not fair
To fade away
No gift to share
To circle blame
How will I fare?
Their callousness has covered me
And now I just don't care
I have to go
I just don't know
Jesus, tell me where

What You Must

You only offer what you must
You only give what you should
You never talk so freely
I can't believe that you would

It hurts me so
It pains me so
I can't believe
You offered my life
It's mine!
While I try to grow

It annoys me so
I can't let go
Of this anger
Now instilled in me!
Now instilled in me!

You've known her for
So long
For so damn long!
And yet I still have reason
For this song!

The End

After an evening of soapbox melodies
I long for my rest as it drifts upon me
I lie in my mind praying for a night of peace
Silence, my friend, drifts down in the end
Each morning I wake I discover my self control
Slide on my brogans, toes find a worn sole
Drift on my way minding all the bills to pay
Goodbye to my friend, praying now for the end

Like a carrot hung in front of a staggering mule
So, my body and mind are awaiting their fuel
Labor all day to put bread on the table
And come back with a check to a hardened home
Don't know if something's missing, don't really care
Got to deal with my problems, sometimes life's not fair
Drinking beer, finger my hair, sitting in my rocking chair
Awaiting my friend, slumber coming in the end

Working the day until it cries out for night
I'm a slave to the dollar, got to give it a fight
Questioning liberty, "Am I free?"
I cry to the sky, "Who's going to save me?"

Yet another evening of crying and hollering
Torn shirts, hard hearts, am I really following
The promise I made before the stakes were weighed?
My Lord, my friend, please come down here and mend
After an evening of praying and memories
I long for my rest as it drifts upon me
With love in my heart I ask for a new start
My Lord, my friend will stay with me to the end

Change of Heart

It's not up to me to change your heart
It's not for personal gain
No matter which way I slice it apart
It just always remains the same

As the workday retreats
And the curtain descends the stage
You think it's time to close your book
Or maybe just turn this page

As the nighttime falls asleep
And the sunlight starts to linger on your face
You wander through the years
Looking to find your place

Hello again, you lost soul of a man
How many calls have you heard
And signs have you seen?
Don't you want to be a child again
And be made clean?

Full Circle

Since that night you yelled at me, I've been feeling small
And so, I couldn't talk to one who didn't trust at all
I found it hard to look at you or smile at any time
I started to wonder the reasons behind my state of mind

And the dialogue ensued and so we felt the wounds anew
We opened up to all the darkness we had to once walk through
We had to share our sorrows about what hurt that night
Just to see the light—just to be the light
Do you wonder why I don't speak to you, why I am so cold?
Do I really have to explain what you shouldn't have to be told?

My heart's been aching to let it go—to let go of all of this
But I just said no—I just said, "No!"
I could not grant it's wish
I yearned to stay identified in my want to stay away
As I had so much anger buried about that fateful day

My heart kept asking
And I answered, "No, I cannot forgive…"
But I stopped this—I had to stop this to truly live
And so, once I sensed the cost in not letting it all go
I wanted to start to stop—start to stop in my saying no
It helped me open up and gave a reason to speak out
And now feeling a strength within me, I didn't have to shout
Amazing how the evening then turned towards the light
And how our talk so turned around
From wrong into so right

Family Tree

The apple doesn't fall far from the tree
I am enslaved, I am not free
The apple doesn't fall far from the tree
I am the apple and I won't see
How to break these chains and be set free
The sins of my fathers are visited on me

Why do I still refuse to see
When all that lies ahead of me
Is revisited lies of generations
Similar passions on different branches
Similar faults and deeper aversions
Similar flames on opposite ends?

Addiction

I Can't Pretend

I know what I hate: it's what I do
And I can't stand up to this monster
This life I've created, torn in two
Commit the act, then run

I can't pretend it's all okay when it isn't anyway
When control is passed all truth is up for grabs
I can't explain it all away when I can't stand today
So, I wallow and pray for this shadow
To leave my house and go away

Plain to See

It may not be the final chapter
Certainly, things lie here after
This is how I feel today
It's not the same as yesterday

Just being human, it's plain to see
That lying in pornography
Is much too much victimization
My eyes are opened, revelation
Now I see it crystal clear
I'm not turned on by it, my dear

It's shades of grey not black and white
Though it looks different, it's not right
Whenever I feel tempted then
I'll just remember this again

Soul Searching

Sometimes I just want to run away
Back into the shadows of yesterday
But deep down, down inside, I know it'll be alright
A little time alone in the dark
I know how it feels to have no spark
I lean back after my game is done
And I wonder why it was so fun

Sometimes the guilt lingers as I cry
I just want to run, I don't know why
But deep down, down inside, it has to be alright
Some days I wish that I could see
How to hate the sin and to become free
Just to see what I mean to you and what you mean to me
Yes, I may ask to be clean and as white as snow
But I already know—

It's all been done before me
Before I was a thought within my parents' minds
My life may lie before me, but in reality
If I go right now, I know what I'll find

Drug

Help break the ice, please cut the cord
To stop this addiction when I am bored
Torn in two, my God, I care
I want you to know I want you here
I see my love going through pain
While the needle I need hovers again
Around the basement calling my name
I ask myself will I feel the same?

You know the drug so quickly now
It hinders my thoughts, you now know how
I won't break free by relying on me
So, I know what to do, I'll rely on you
Commit to you and open my life
Seeing you there with a knife
Don't cut my heart, I will fall back
Because I can't stand under attack

You helping me back, you be my love?
You helping me to kick this drug?
Please say it now, dream open love
You helping me to kick this drug?

Casting Away a Silent Death

Beastly figures are here moving through
The landscape of this war-battered world
Over the hills of long-forgotten yesterdays, throwing ideas into my brain
Endlessly hoping to rechannel my thoughts to rattle my chains
To remake my name so that I may forget my chosen path

No time to doubt or give credit to the authority or influence in use
The world won't stay together without my needle
No diplomacy here, no kingdom come, no angels from above
Only the debased beautifier, only the bowman
A callous thumb with another arrow, holding back no longer
Time to diminish the pain, to enhance my brain with more nightmares
The old one was by yesterday, and lucifer the day before
He'll be here with old nick, knocking down my door
That hellhound won't go far

This figure of death embodies much more
Encloaked in deceit, destruction, and fear
Knowing I'm isolated, making a path with sulfurous smoke, filling the air!
Making it unbreathable, choking to death, no air, no air!
Searching for the heavens, veering for the sky
Pockets of air nowhere to be found
I struggle, fighting off, searching, grasping, convulsing
Getting closer to my Maker, I proclaim a quick prayer

Shattering these nightmares, and casting death away
As chanting becomes silence, so despair becomes hope
Dispersing destruction, deceit, and fear embodied within
This demonic litany passing away as quickly as it appeared
Only to be shrouded by a silent hope and a little fear

Life & Self

Life's to Live

Is life a treasure?
Is life a gift?
Your life broke down?
You need a lift?
Is life a farce?
Is life a game?
Your life's a goal?
Is mine the same?

Is life a war?
Is life a test?
God knows we'll know
Just like all the rest
Is life a question?
Or just a quest?
Is life just life?
We do our best?

Is life a pleasure?
Or a trial of pain?
Is life a sanity?
Or just insane?
Is life to take?
Or all to give?
Maybe it's just
That life's to live

I Am Because

The conflict, the thoughts, the paradox
The reasons, the motives, the cost
The mind games I play with myself, in my way
The line that's crossed

The hope, the love, the faith we share
The doubt, the pain, and the hate
The heart I hold near is the one that's in here
I've slaughtered fate

The woman, a friend, a part of me
I see her heart and I pray
The agreements we make aren't promises to break
Yesterday, tomorrow, today

The game, the hunt, the race we run
The worries, the fear, and the loss
The limited facts, the unspoken acts
And unforeseen costs

I cannot deny what I have here inside me
I cannot forget that I am so real
I cannot let go of all I seem to be
I cannot be all that I'd like to be
I cannot steer clear of the lies that are me
I cannot clear up all the pain that I cause
I cannot forget that I am confusion
I cannot see clear who I am because

A Brand-New Day

The skies have cleared, and the rain is gone
The night is over, and the sun has shone
The morning's come, and breakfast is served
And now I've got what is deserved
The clouds are white, and the sky is blue
And now I'm happy since I have you
All that what was has passed away
Tomorrow's here, a brand-new day

My Love

Indecision seems to weigh on me
Like a mighty fist overpowering me
Just like a heavy hand holding me
I'm just a twig and so I'll snap
Am I a man? I'll just collapse
Can my emotions bridge this synapse?
Into my life, departing my heart
Oh, how I pray for this to start
They say a man who draws a chart
On where to dig, and digs some more
He might just find some iron ore
And so, I go just fighting for
My love

Just a Pawn

I'd like to not look back
But the slides keep reappearing
And appearing before my eyes
Always forming on the screen
And I'm just a pawn

I'd like to not see the past
But it rings again at my door
And knocks it down to the ground
And my home is now destroyed
And I'm just a pawn

I'm hoping to forget what was
But life just continues
On the merry way it has
Until it leaves me alone
And I'm just a pawn

Take a Stand

Time to break out, time to run free
Get out of torture into the liberty
Covered by the dark shroud it looks so light
When surrounded by wrong all things seem right
Time to fess up, time to confess
Put on your true clothes, get out of that dress
It's not time to sway, use all your might
Stand up for what you believe and fight

There are certain rules to live your life, certain laws
You got to stand with the criticism as well as with the applause

Sometimes there's more action behind the scenes than on the stage
The red curtain covers all, all your anger, all your rage
Don't keep it covered too long, there is a war to wage
Don't be deceived and trapped within this gilded cage

No More

Just keep me running from one tragedy the next
Just keep me moving, tomorrow's will be the best
Just keep me going from one holocaust to another
And I pray that it won't bother me no more

I find my own way of making time work for me
I'm finding my own life and I'm looking for I.D.
From today to tomorrow I don't know how far to go
And so, I can't let go no more

And the drum beat of my youth has died out once again
And the tambourine of my happiness is no longer my friend
I must make my life scream, make my world tremble
From the chaos which surrounds me
It won't surround me no more

Times to Turn

So, I'm standing still and looking back
Standing still, no reaction
So, I'm standing still, it's a fact
I'm not moving, but I know that
These are times to turn
But I don't know if these are times to learn
But all I know is these are times

My heart may say one thing
But my feet are walking away
The thoughts within my mind I can't stand
I'm not moving, but I know that
These are times to turn
But I don't know if these are times to learn
But all I know is these are times

So, adversity rears its ugly face
I try for a smile to take its place

Dipping My Feet

Dipping my feet little bit in the water
Dipping my ears, arms, eyes, nose, legs
Dripping my body all over from the water
Dripping my life, is it ever going to change?

These bones that I carry one moment to another
Are just my baggage on this flight
To a place I may lay my burdens down
Through all this wrong I still know right

These stones that I hold one day to another
Are now my weight and so my life
While in this world I stay so wet
I still feel cold, so I don't sweat

Until Tomorrow

Somehow, I see
That my life could be
Very healthy
And free

Somehow, I feel
That I could deal
With what is real
I steal

My time away until tomorrow
My life today, I hope to borrow
My soul is sunk in loss and sorrow
Until it comes
Until tomorrow comes

Take the Time

Why am I so dependent on the writing of my thoughts?
Why am I judge and jury and the victim in these courts?
Why do I fear the lack thereof, inactive pencil, uncaring hand?
Why don't I take the time to understand?

So, as the story goes
I wish to see the end right now
I walk the path I chose
I'm walking

I guess I'm fearful
That this gift might just leave and not come back
Might just leave me
With all I lack

The Hidden

At times like this, why I feel this way
Stuck between two worlds and the dues that we all pay
Closing my closets, don't let my skeletons run free
Caught between the fear that I hide and my so-called liberty

Away from you but you are so close to me
All I ever see, I chose to see, are doors into slavery
There's a wall between us, I've built this wall before
You're always waiting for me, I have no courage to open that door

Well friend, you know what I say but you can't see what I mean
Thought I'd keep it welled-up inside my heart, don't let nobody see
Ever since I was a little boy, I held my light inside of me
How could I throw it all out the door, when I could have had it abundantly?

Little Reminders

Little reminders of how it used to be
Pass in front of me only to help me see
That it isn't that way anymore

Many memories of how it once was
Pass before my mind only to help me know
That it isn't that way anymore

And we all seem to be creatures of habit
And we all tend to feel good until we don't have it
And we all find this common thread
Circling over in our heads
Until we open our eyes to see just how it is
And what our life has become

Little reminders of how it is now
Circle me all the time only to prove to me
That there is a new horizon

Many thoughts of how it is right now
Chain me to the table and force me to eat
Of the fruit that now surrounds me

And familiarity only continues to prove to me
That I just don't care if it is this way
And what encompasses me now is not the past
And I see my life in all its glory
While opening my eyes to see just how it is
And what my life has become

Stones That I Carry

Take my time, don't be shy
Seal my fate, steal and lie
Holy water, sacred blood
Time and again, return to mud
In-between, up and down
Take the turn, round and round
Behind, before, spin some more
But I can't hear the knock on the door
Lie around and open the box
Peeping-tom, pick the locks
Running scared, tried and true
And when I'm sad, return to You

So, I wonder what's important to me
And I wonder why I can't see
And I wonder if I am free
From the stones that I carry?

My Home

My mind is like a grave of ideals
My spirit wanting to know where they went
Don't really know what I should feel
Am I really sure what's fake and what's real?
Just want to live life day to day
Amazing how life can get this way

So cold, so alone, deep down I know my home
In a valley of snow and ice
Just backsliding down, you know it ain't nice
So cold, so alone, I want to go back to my home

My life fades behind closed doors
My closest friends don't notice the change
I got to live in love, stay true to the cause
I just got to try, just got to try again
Taking advantage of this gift I've been given
Oh Lord, how can I love this life I'm living?

Gull

There's a gull on a pole and it's just looking around
Its eyes reflecting the setting sun
Think it's bored, think it's dumb for sitting in the sun?
My thoughts reflecting the lonely one

Other gulls flying by don't stop to wonder why
Their eyes just facing horizon's way
Between the world of the air, of the sea, of the sky
My thoughts looking towards another day

Without the gull on the pole moving its head back and forth
There is no time to stay outside, I wonder why
The bird is gone, and so my song won't be lasting very long
My thoughts have left, I stare and sigh
Just like the gull on the pole, my world goes by

Epitaph

There comes a time when mountains fall
And solid cliffs are moved away
I'm being honest, accept my word
There is no one else to support what I say
I am torn from the tent where I lived secure
I am dragged off unwillingly to face king death
My brothers and sisters won't come near me
And my wife can't stand the smell of my breath

I will happily call the grave my father
And the worms that eat me, my sisters and mother
With a chisel carve my words in stone
And record my rebel, my complaint, my groan

Slipping Away

"Men at ease have contempt for misfortune
as the fate of those whose feet are slipping"

Would a wise man answer with empty notions?
Or fill his belly with the hot east wind?
Have you had your fill of those potent potions?
It's time for all to confess they've sinned

Your maxims are proverbs of ashes
Your defenses are defenses of clay
In the dark you say, "light is near!"
You turn the night into the day
It's like revealing the things of darkness
Bringing deep shadows into the day
When life get rough and times get tough
You're just slipping away

See the day of my birth and the night it was said
"A boy is born!" Why wasn't it dead?
Each and every man's life is but a breath
Show me my end, show me my death
We were sent to stagger through a trackless waste
As mountains erode and move from their place

Feel at Home

Here I am again sitting at the beach
Where sweaters have replaced bathing suits
And flags don't fly no more
Dunes are fading, bathrooms closed
It's just cold comfort that places like this exist
To soothe the soul
And make me feel at home

Some relief holds true here in my life
Something's clear and near understanding
I'm happy that this place I love
Is going through what I am too
A lack of housekeeping
And an old fire now cold
And that in this world I'm not alone

Now although the place I rest my head
Is not the place I rest my soul
My life, though empty, remains full
For in this place I can rest
And I can find myself and You
Find myself in You to soothe my soul
And make me feel at home

Time Passes

Time passes, my life maneuvers
To embody the wind of change
Life passes, time maneuvers
But under it all we stay the same

As I sit here all alone
I notice the change in my life
I bury my face within my hands
And stare into the cold silence
It's freezing in the winter
The summer the heat is on
Getting sick from every degree
As I sit here all alone

I can feel the temperature changing
I can feel my life rearranging

I sit with a friend
I feel the warmth of the room
There's also tension in the air
I feel the warmth of the room
You've been too far away
Just beyond my grasp
Turning before me
Are you there?

In the Dark

Sometimes I feel like flying
Hanging onto eagle's wings
Sometimes I feel like walking
Taking a stand on firmer things
God will be my guide, always by my side
With my head in the clouds and my feet on the ground
I'll wander around
Until I'm found

I found what I found, and I know what I know
I may care about you but I've a life of my own
You're the one that closed the door and so I hung up my hat
But I've found what I found and that's not where I'm at

In the womb I'll stay, in this place I'll pray
For my spirit's conceived but my heart's away
I'll pray to the Lord although my heart's still torn
Between two worlds, still soon reborn

Why do I feel led to the dark?
As God is my guide in the dark
My works don't change what happens here
Since God is my light in the dark

The Edge of an Oasis

Like a rose which is grown on the edge of an oasis
It faces the desert and longs to be held
By the sweltering heat
But it cannot draw much closer
Than the way it chooses to face

No matter what it knows
It tries to leave
The spot where it grows
It wants to believe
That it's all a mirage
And every now and then
It looks back to see
The life-giving oasis
And thinks, "I can always be
Near the water when I need to be"

The only thing it refuses to see
Is that what it has cannot be changed day-after-day
Because it is planted, he is planted for all to see
On the edge of salvation and insanity

Like the rose I was planted on the edge of an oasis
Facing the desert

I'm Calling You

In the beginning, the miracle
That made me to see the revelation
That there exists a time when I could be free
Only my beginning, my time, only my life and my way
The calling of my heart into this everlasting love

In the middle, my denial
My turning away from the word
The disillusion that was illusion
The blinding darkness that enveloped this fervor, this miracle
So, turning from You, from this love, I still knew the truth

In the end, acceptance
And my understanding that it doesn't depend on me
And no matter what I may do, I'm loved, and I'll love You forever
Since a freedom exists as I'm still waiting for Your coming back
And for today my heart is at rest and I'm calling You

The World

In the World

There is disruption, corruption, confusion, and disgrace
Dreams deferred, ashes, dust, anger, war, and toxic waste
A fight for peace, release, birth destroyed by death
Long lines, no time, you're just fallen like the rest
No value of life, add strife to this fabulous melting pot
High priced gas, broken glass, who fired the first shot?
Long streams of tears, forgotten years, and no one really cares
A loud cry, a sigh, nothing left but despair
Aborted lives, reborn lies, grim pictures torn apart
We left no trace of open space, we left no horse near the cart
Images old, we are bold, nostalgic flags are now unfurled
No sacrifice, we're cold-as-ice. Is there any hope left for this world?
In my sailing ship upon the sea, in the world
God help me if the water gets within

Any One Man

Little Jimmy went off to school just like the day before
He walked out of his house but he don't want to go no more
There's no life left as he walks down the street
His books on his shoulders and no soles on his feet

Young Mary went off to work just like yesterday
She got caught up in politics at the workplace, it's okay
She stumbles as she steps to her station on the floor
But she knows very well she can't take any more
Souls in anguish and souls in pain
Can any one man alleviate the strain?

Middle-aged Sally has been looking around for a very long time
She needs something to fill this need deep, deep down inside
You know she runs to sex, then to booze, and last to drugs
She's still looking for someone to get her out of that hole she dug
Souls in torture and souls do strain
Can any one man alleviate the pain?

Michael, the new born man, sits inside his cluttered head
Studying his favorite bands lyrics while lying on his bed
He doesn't know the music has taken control of his mind
Because he's never lived without this desire, this fire to find
Souls in mastery and pain does stay
Can any one man please take it away?

Jed, the corporate lawyer, sees a warped picture for sure
Every day, while going to work, he steps over the homeless on the floor
Although he thinks the answers are inside his head
Little does he know he's the warped one instead
Souls oblivious and don't realize
Can any one man open up our eyes?

Index

1 to 2	50	Day One	12
		Day Two	27
		Dipping My Feet	135
About It	88	Drug	124
About Me	99		
About You	2		
All I Own	16	Edge of an Oasis, The	148
All My Songs	83	Emotions That We Hold	106
All the Rest	59	End, The	116
All the Same	112	Epitaph	143
Alone	23		
Always with Me	5		
Any One Man	152	Family Tree	119
April Fool	63	Feel at Home	145
As I Am?	33	Freedom and Indifference	44
At Ease	98	Full Circle	118
Away	31		
		Go with Me	86
Back for More	49	Gratitude Song	3
Best That I Can, The	10	Gull	142
Bitter Pill, The	25		
Blue Cross, Silver Chain	105		
Brand-New Day, A	129	Having You	20
Burdens We Share, The	69	Heal Thyself	29
By His Wounds	82	Her	65
		Hidden, The	138
		Hollow	57
Carefree	9	How, Why or What From	14
Casting Away a Silent Death	125	Hurt	113
Change of Heart	117		
Changes	52		
Closer to Me	66		

I Am Because	128	Needs	107
I Can't Pretend	121	New Beginning, A	87
I Don't Need	108	New Birth of Tomorrow, The	76
I Evade, I Discover	96	No More	133
I Love You	4	No One Knows	58
I Tremble	19	Northern Outlook	28
I'm Calling You	149		
In Duress	40		
In the Dark	147	On My Mind	67
In the World	151	Our Time Together	26
Insecurity	62		
Interest	100		
It Must Be You	55	Painstaking, Still Questioned	48
		Place	78
		Plain to See	122
Jesus, Tell Me Where	114	Plow through Time	60
Judas Love	72	Put Me to Bed	35
Just a Pawn	131		
Just a Stone's Throw Away	87		
		Quo Vadis	92
Learning to Walk	80		
Leave the Romance	61	Renewal	81
Let Me Know	95	Road to Return, The	8
Letters from Holland	53		
Letting Go of All That I Know	47		
Life's to Live	127		
Little Reminders	139		
Midnight Clear, A	103		
My Guitar Nearby	17		
My Home	141		
My Love	130		
My Love's Been Crucified	36		
My Soul	85		
My World	101		

Sensing but Apart	34
Sincerely, Your Friend	104
Slipping Away	144
So I See	30
Solace Now	38
Soul Searching	123
Speechless	6
Stay (This Memory)	64
Stones That I Carry	140
Strength Perfected	89
Sweetness of the Moment, The	24
Sword of the Lamb, The	94
Take a Stand	132
Take the Time	137
Taking the Turn	109
Talk to You	90
Talk with God	79
Temper Me	7
Test of Time	93
That Place, Called Home	15
These Memories of You	18
This	42
Time Passes	146
Times to Turn	134
To Meet with You	75
Today with You	56
Tour Guide	11
Transfiguration, The	74
Treasures	70
Trust in Him	73
Two Bodies, One Spirit	21
Until Tomorrow	136
Until We Meet Again	110
Waiting for You	91
Walk by Faith	77
Wayside	51
What I Won't Do	45
What Senselessness Is	41
What You Must	115
Whatever You Might Think	46
Where to Go from Here	13
Who Could Ask for More?	39
Will Grow in Time	32
Without You	37
Yesterday Again	71
You're My Friend	102

www.ingramcontent.com/pod-product-compliance
Lightning Source LLC
LaVergne TN
LVHW011421080426
835512LV00005B/185